NOT YOUR AVERAGE BABYMAMA

HOW TO MANAGE CO-PARENTING

IRENE ESTRADA

© 2021 Irene Estrada

All rights reserved. No portion of this book may be reproduced in any form without permission from the Author. For permissions contact:

NotYourAverageBabymama1@gmail.com

To the three that made me a Mother and gave me the challenge of my life.
God, Chucky, &
Xavier, I love you

TABLE OF CONTENTS

The Purpose   vii
My Story   xi

Your "Child's Father" is the new "BabyDaddy."	1
New Goals, New You!	5
Emotional & Personal Development	9
The See-Through Veil	15
No crop circles = No signs	19
Set the Tone	23
Petty is as Petty Does	27
Look Who's Dating Now	33
Your Child's Best Advocate	39
Stop! In the Name of Love for Your Child	43
Work Smarter, Not Harder	47
Ask and Tell	51
Co-Parenting Haven	57
Never-Ending Parenthood	59

The Purpose

IT WOULD BE AWESOME if you could decide that you and your child's father could part ways and be in co-parenting heaven for the next, however many years until your child turns 18. It would be fabulous if you both could not be petty, resentful, angry, or determined to make the rest of each other's lives a living hell. That isn't always the case; that's why I felt the need to write this book. It is always unsettling when I hear family or friends behaving childishly or selfishly when interacting with their child's father or mother. I can't be the only one. I've seen too many parents on television saying or doing harmful things to their lifelong partner in parenting in front of the children; it is hugely detrimental to their child's growth and well-being. Every conversation with coworkers or clients about making better decisions for their child's sake is getting worrisome. Overhearing the woman on the bus yelling at her child's father on the phone or seeing a father disrespecting his child's mother right in front of the child is no longer unbelievable. We have so many advances in science, technology, and even space exploration in this day and age. Still, most have not matured enough to responsibly handle adult interaction with a person they are no longer in a "relationship with," which frequently leaves a beautiful innocent bystander they created to become a pawn in their war of exes.

My purpose for this book is to help change the way you think about co-parenting, your child's father, and your expectations for the situation as a whole. In doing so, you will be able to set your eyes on having a lighthearted and purposeful life. I want you to start opening your mind to the idea of shedding some of the layers of your current state of being—to become the leader in the partnership of parenthood. I want you to see yourself as more than just the average BabyMama. The standard idea of what being a BabyMama entails has long been set. I want moms to take themselves out of the BabyMama mindset completely. I intend to make it easier for you to have a strictly friendly/drama-free relationship with your child's father. Maybe not at first, but it can happen. My intention is for you to be so good at getting yourself on the right track that you might even inspire your child's father to follow your lead.

Most importantly, if he doesn't follow your lead. I want you to accept that you can still bring peace and focus to your life and happiness to your child. I have over 17 years of personal experience with co-parenting and more than 20 years of watching many people do it wrong—and right, sometimes. I'm offering you the possibility to get it correct for yourself. Some topics I will put more emphasis on because we need to go in! Some topics are pretty straightforward.

As of day, your starting point in co-parenting may be that you are recently single, or you may already be in the middle of the co-parenting struggle. Take this journey with me. I will tell you a little about my personal experience with the topics we cover, although this is not an autobiography. I'm going to share with you how I handled the tug of war that co-parenting can be. How I wished I would have dealt with it and how I managed things once I knew better. As they say, "when you know better, do better."

In most cases, we just weren't taught the best practices for dealing with an ex that you share a child with. We end up with so many blurred lines that not only are we confused about our relationship with our ex, so are the children. No one can move forward with their lives when they feel stuck and don't have direction. Let's be unstuck together! I will make suggestions for you to think, be, speak, and believe differently. Be yourself but with boundaries that will help you take charge. They say that any person shouldn't tie themselves to a partner until they have found themselves and their purpose, which makes perfect sense, right! Once you find your purpose in life, you may end up on a completely different path than you were, and now the people and places in your life may not fit into where you want to go. In our case, we already have a child, and we are connected to an ex. So our decision-making process has to be made with those things in mind. That is where some of that stuck feeling may have come from. Becoming a mother changes your life; it doesn't end it. There are still decisions you can make to loosen the ties you have to your child's father. Making good decisions on your behalf is what will give you some freedom. You will be amazed at how lighthearted and purposeful you will feel when you put down some of the burdens you are carrying. Let's start with me, telling you a little about myself and my co-parenting journey.

My Story

MY NAME IS IRENE, and I am the mother of a 17-year-old young man named Xavier(X). His father and I knew each other for about three months as friends and were in a relationship for five months when I became pregnant. Two months before I knew I was pregnant, I realized that my son's father was not who he said he was, and he was not going to be that man anytime soon. I asked him if he would be willing to improve the problems we had. He agreed, but not much changed. I decided to end the relationship. When I found out I was pregnant. I told him, and he wanted us to try to work things out. I decided that I owed it to our unborn child to do my best to try and create a happy home for him.

No matter how unrealistic it felt at the time. I was determined to make the best of the situation. Looking back as an older and wiser adult, I should have cut my losses. We experienced an additional year and a half of headache, disappointment, and stress. That drama caused us to break up for the last time; my son was eight months old. I was tired of taking on most of the responsibility, and we could never see eye to eye. His father had issues that had nothing to do with me, and he wasn't working on them. We both loved our son, but we didn't function as a team for him. I wanted his father to meet me where I was, and he wanted the same. Instead, we should have been meeting in the middle.

As time went on, I realized that I was hard on his father because he didn't make every effort to put our son first, and he didn't sacrifice for him as I did. Those things frustrated me, disappointed me, and made me disrespect him as a man… and as a father. Once I lose respect for a person, I can admit that I don't treat them well. In most cases, I remove them from my life. In this case, I wanted him in our son's life. I gave him opportunities to redeem himself, but in my eyes, he didn't. He continued to sink lower on the list of things I felt mattered. I couldn't see any value in him as a father.

After a couple of years apart, I began to spend less of my time focusing on trying to make him a better father. I realized that I couldn't help him if I didn't help me first. So I refocused on myself. I intentionally learned to look at things differently by not taking things personally and seeing the bright side of situations. I was 21 at the time, and looking back, I realize even as a mature 21-year old. I didn't have the patience I needed for the situation. I looked at myself and saw the things I wanted to change. I thought about who I was before becoming a mom. What kind of person did I want to be? What improvements could I make with myself as a woman and as a Mother? I learned so much about myself and was determined to have patience with my personal growth.

One of the books that helped me was 'The Secret.' Living a joyous life with positive thoughts, having optimistic expectations, and making moves as if everything was moving and working in my favor. I eventually used my new positive way of thinking and reacting to benefit my relationship with X's dad. We started to communicate better and share more responsibilities. When X was around three years old, his dad made more efforts; we even got to talk about why we didn't work out without arguing. It was refreshing to speak to him and not have him deny the bad decisions he made. When my son's father expressed his frustration with how cold I became toward him, I got to tell him I was never in love with him. I was in love with who he said he was. He acknowledged his fault in that, and we came to agree that our son would be our only concern moving forward. That was such a relief!

As time went on, I became more patient with him because I realized that even though he was not the dad I wanted him to be to our son, he was trying. He's human, just like me, and no one is perfect. It wasn't always peaceful, but it wasn't stressful anymore. He would go through times where he made wrong decisions on behalf of X and wanted me to co-sign him. I refused, and it would cause conflict, but I don't regret my choices. My only concern is my son's well-being. If anyone makes terrible decisions that will affect X's happiness, I will not co-sign that. That includes his father. When X was about 6, I sent him to his father's house for Spring break. While he was there, his father and I argued over the phone, and he stated I could not talk to X because I did not respect him. My son's father was right; I still didn't respect him. Although we made things work, I didn't respect him for not seeing X as often as he should, not paying enough child support, not paying it consistently, and not being a good role model. Still, that did not make it ok to prevent me from talking to my son because of what I thought of his father.

Long story short, it turned out that the real reason he didn't put X on the phone was that X had gotten hurt while playing with a cousin around his age. He didn't want X to tell me about it. I know now that although it was his responsibility to tell me. I didn't make it easy for him to tell me such a thing. Our communication still wasn't the best; my yelling about his faults every chance I got was not going to make him open to speaking freely—all of this led to a series of Petty acts. After already feeling like he was an unnecessary headache, I admit, having to also deal with his constantly changing level of commitment was aggravating. I was infuriated with him for not allowing me to speak to my son. I got myself together and got into mom mode and put X first. When the time came to get my son, I calmly grabbed my son's hand and gathered his things.

The next day I called his dad and told him I would no longer be putting up with the stress and frustration he caused me and with the disappointment and misguided leadership he offered to our son. I made the sacrifices; I sat in the ER at midnight. I took off from work to be at the school plays, paid for the childcare, and put the clothes on his back. Fulfilling his broken promises became my burden. I refused to be told that I couldn't speak to my son by the man who didn't fulfill his role but wanted my respect. I told him to take me to court to set up visitation and take parenting classes if he wanted to be in his son's life. He never did.

When X asked for his father, I would tell him that his dad

had some things he needed to do to be in his life. He loves him very much, but unfortunately, he has yet to do them. When he does, he will be back in his life. It was not easy for him or any of us.

His father and I were in contact off and on, and he would ask to see X but would not make any changes. He still had the same combative personality and was cursing all the time. Two years later, his father had a different attitude. He wanted to do better for our son and agreed to stop trying to come in between X and me. I allowed him to talk to him on the phone for months. I made sure to listen to their conversations with the phone on speaker to ensure there were no adverse or stressful conversations being had with X. He and I had come to have better communication. He was also making better decisions. His father showed me that they were rooted in doing the best for our son. He asked me if he could come to our son's 9th birthday party, and I agreed. He and his whole family came. X was delighted and overjoyed to see them. X became very emotional when it came time for his father to leave. The three of us spoke, I agreed to let him back in X's life full-time. He decided that he would commit to being a better father and respect me for always being a committed Mother. Since then, we have worked together for our son's benefit.

I am not going to lie to you. It was hard to accept X's father for who he is. It was harder to admit to myself that I am the rock in X's life. Even if he is doing much more for X now, he isn't doing as much as I do as a parent. It was tough to accept that, although we both played our part in bringing a person into this world. The responsibilities and the weight of trying to make him into the best man and person he can be are not equal. Although it was hard, I accepted that I could no longer try to get him to be the kind of father I wanted my son to have, but I could be the best mom I could be. Since he was now ready to do better, I would have patience with his growth as I did with mine. I had to acknowledge that my son will love his father unconditionally. That was the kind of boy we raised, and I was going to respect their relationship. There are things that my son expects of me that he doesn't expect from his father. I would let him decide what he needed from his father but made sure his father knew what I expected of him. I expected him to guide our son in the right direction, be the best role model he could...or at least be X's voice of reason for what not to do, love him unconditionally, and help me teach him how to be a responsible, honest, kind-hearted, well-functioning and capable man. He's only 17 years old, but he is well on his way.

After thinking about how far my son's father and I have come, I wanted to share it with you. There were plenty of things I left out because we would be here all day. What I wanted you to know is that I am not perfect, and I've been there and done that. The goal is never to be perfect but to do better. I learned a lot along the way. I'm not telling you to do what I did but to learn from it. My experience has taught me so much about patience, acceptance, fear, expectations, pettiness, and starting over. I believe that we can all learn from the experience of others. As a Mother, you may be going through a lot, whether with your child's father or just in life. It can get overwhelming, frustrating, and it may be hard to think that there is anything that you can do to change things around. I wish I never played a part in separating my son from his dad. I also know that everything happens for a reason. As a mom, sometimes you're the "bad guy"; bad things happen, and we have to make hard decisions.

Good things can come out of it as they did in our case. Life can get better, and Co-parenting can be manageable. I do not promise any miracles because the tips I offer in this book take time and effort. Make an effort, be the bigger person, grow, focus, have patience, think outside the box, and believe that things are moving and working in your favor. It is worth it! I was committed to doing all the work upfront to have a longer stretch of peace along the way. Some people feel like it's too much to make an effort upfront, but you are just making your hard times longer if you don't.

My passion is in helping people grow. I believe I am here to plant seeds and watch them grow on their own. These tips are seeds that I am hoping to plant in your mind and your heart. Meditate on the ones you are ready for now and take the necessary steps to improve. Self-improvement takes time. Be patient with yourself, and even if you give in to the temptation of your old ways today, start fresh tomorrow. Be patient with your child's father. That may sound impossible right now, but there is a light at the end of the tunnel. Don't be afraid to lead the way.

1

YOUR "CHILD'S FATHER" IS THE NEW "BABYDADDY."

I would like you to take a moment to read the two descriptions listed below. Say both phrases out loud.

BabyDaddy

Child's Father

If you think to yourself and imagine you are hearing someone else say each of them. I want you to picture the kind of person you feel would be saying both of them. I'm not referring to ethnicity. I want you to think about their education level, what kind of lifestyle they live, and how they carry themselves.

Does one of them reflect a positive image? If so, incorporate this new verbiage into your vocabulary. Mission accomplished!

"BabyDaddy" isn't usually associated with a responsible, logical, bright, or focused on doing what is best for his child kind of man. Maybe you're just joking around by calling him that. Why call your child's father something you don't want him to be? Give him the kind of title that will promote him being the kind of man you want him to be to your child. A father is a guide and teacher, a protector of the children they bring into this world. Fathers try to do what's right, not the most comfortable thing. A father is patient with his children and thinks of creative ways to connect with them. The book is only titled with BabyMama because a lot of people identify with it. Repeat after me: my son's father, my daughter's father. It's not a hard transition to change your vocabulary. Change what you call him, and you might start seeing him differently.

Mission 2, Referring to yourself as a BabyMama doesn't represent your worth. This title is associated with a woman who has a baby with a man that she is no longer in a relationship with, but she won't let him go. The BabyMama is also determined to make the child's father miserable by any means necessary. Some people use it as a title for being the mother of a child and choose not to associate it with any negative background. That doesn't stop you from misrepresenting yourself when referring to yourself that way. BabyMamas use child support as a means to get their hair done or spend the money irresponsibly. They go on Maury to find out who the father of their baby is. If you have done any of these things, you are reading this book because you are ready to be more than that. You are now the child's mother. You are not the average BabyMama! You will no longer fit the description of the average anything. As the child's mother, you carry yourself with dignity! You use child support and any resources you have wisely for your child's well-being. You accept that the relationship with your child's father is over and that your focus is now solely on the child and improving your life. Even if people know you to be the average BabyMama and can't see you are more than that, you can continue to grow in this new perspective. Let them think whatever they want about you. You are allowed to start over. We can be anything we want to be; some things just take more effort. Start by making an effort not to refer to yourself or your child's father in a way that misrepresents the both of you.

2

NEW GOALS, NEW YOU!

So, you are no longer with your child's father. Whether this is a relief or a shock to your system, it's a great time to figure out what you will do next. Believe it or not, you are a changed woman. If you're not, you should be. Every relationship should be a learning experience. There is something that your child's father taught you. Whether it was to stop having one-night stands, that you're insecure, and it resulted in him taking off, that you just need to stick to your first mind and end harmful interactions with men as soon as they start, etc.—it taught you something. Take some time to figure out the things he kept saying that may have been true. Especially things that other people tell you about yourself. Take some time to be single. You need it and deserve it. Singleness is not a punishment. It's the perfect time to focus on you. Get back on track with the goals you let fall to the side while trying to be his superwoman. Do some meditation, catch up with your friends, go to the gym, take a class, or start that business. Write down the things you haven't gotten over and make a point to work on overcoming them.

Ex's come into your life for a reason. They could be a reflection of something that needs work within you. I see them as God's way of helping you see the error of your ways, so you don't continuously make the same mistakes and to better prepare you for your future significant other. If you don't work on yourself now, you will still be Miss Wrong when you meet your lifetime companion. They will not deal with the nonsense that you will be bringing to their peace. With every bad habit that you break, you will be closer to being the new you. I am challenging you to write down the top three things you think you need to work on for the next three months. Studies have shown that it takes three weeks to form a habit. Take one month to work on one thing at a time so as not to overwhelm yourself.

Goal Setting:

Write down the top three things you know you need to work on below.

These can be habits like, "Being one time," or if you are already in another relationship: "I make other people a priority over my mate." "Being petty when I don't want to express that I'm feeling hurt."

1.

2.

3.

Write down the steps you will take to resolve the bad habits above and write down why it's important to you. E.g., "I will set alarms on my phone for upcoming events because I want to be a woman of my word." "I will make sure I tell people how I feel to avoid being petty because I hate regretting hurting people that are important to me."

A.

B.

C.

It's a proven fact that you are more likely to remember things when you write them down. Take this part seriously. Write down your goals. Come back to this in a month and see if you have used opportunities that presented themselves to do better. Small changes make the big picture. Have you ever painted a picture and then got up close, taking in the little details, and the image seemed off? When you take a step back and see it from a distance, you realize it looks excellent and flows pretty well. These small changes may not seem like they are important or will make a difference in the long run. Once you have put them in place and they become a norm, you'll see how without them, the picture wouldn't be complete. These goals are steps that will lead you in the right direction. In turn, they will help your relationship with your child's father.

3

EMOTIONAL & PERSONAL DEVELOPMENT

Be focused on being your best "whole self." This part is not about comparing yourself to others, it's not about tearing yourself down, and it's not about looking at your flaws with a microscope. It's about figuring out what you want for your future and projecting that out to the world in every way that you can. Live the life you want to have. Look, plan, speak, think, feel, and be the you that you desire. Small steps in the right direction will lead to a new you further down the road. Take some time to think about the things below.

How are you feeling mentally and emotionally? Do you feel stressed? What is causing that stress? These areas are something you need to identify. Do you feel depressed? What is bringing on that feeling? What healthy things do you think you need to do to feel relieved from the depression? Do them!

Think of healthy, productive things that make you feel great, and enjoy them. What makes you smile? Do something that will bring happiness to your life. Have you considered getting some counseling? Having a professional whom you can talk to may help you open your mind to new possibilities. They can also help you see the things that are under the surface.

Whether you want to make a plan to buy clothes that make you feel fabulous or if you're going to stop cursing because the kind of future you want doesn't involve doing that (I had to do this because I was a potty mouth), it is all doable with time. I feel the need to mention that personal and emotional development is something you should work on before entering the dating world. Think of yourself better and know what you want for yourself and your child's future. By doing that, you are more likely to realize what kind of partner is right for you and ignore the wrong ones. Some things may be harder to get over; for example, you may have been continuously cheated on or have a hard time trusting people. No matter what the hardships were, you deserve better. The fact that you have lived through those difficulties proves that you are a strong woman. You deserve a strong partner who will respect and love you. So, take this time to become your best self.

Personal and emotional development is crucial for us to talk about because we witness too many women engaging in relationships before they are ready. They have these random men around their children. Some people begin relationships for the wrong reasons. They enter relationships because they only think of what they can get from the situation, they are lonely, or they will be with any man who wants them because they don't think they have any options. It ends up being a vicious cycle. A guy hurts you, now you don't care, and you go and break someone else's heart. It's upsetting to see people do this to each other. Dating usually leads to relationships. Ultimately, good relationships lead to caring, love, and trust. When one of you isn't ready for that, it can tear the other person apart. I am not only blaming the person that did the hurting because, in some cases, they tell you, "I am not looking for anything serious." Since you are intensely interested in this person, you can't hear the words coming out of their mouth. That doesn't mean they didn't say it or that they aren't showing you something different than they said. Sometimes in our immaturity, inexperience, and wishful thinking, we make excuses for people. We need to bend the truth to feel better about the situation. *"He wants to be with me. He's just seeing that other girl because he's afraid of getting hurt."* We can easily convince ourselves of things like that to comfort ourselves, which keeps us stuck in naivety.

Emotional intelligence is reading people's emotions, using emotions to express yourself, and understanding others' feelings. Most importantly, it's about regulating your own emotions to adjust to each situation and understanding that the emotions the other person is projecting usually have nothing to do with you. Being emotionally intelligent is believed to be a significant contributor to overall success in life. The missing factor we don't talk much about is how often people's emotions or the things that stem from their emotions like facial expressions, body language, tone of voice, and choice of words have absolutely nothing to do with us. Think about how many times you had a rough morning and since you didn't learn to control your emotions. Your behavior for the rest of the day was rude, disrespectful, and unnecessary. How many times did situations escalate because you were mad at one person but blamed it on everyone else? How many arguments have you had with your child's father stemming from him crossing his arms when he talked to you, you rolling your eyes at him, or sucking your teeth? Those are actions that happened because they are an outward expression of your emotions.

Some people love that expression that says: If you don't take me at my worst, you don't deserve me at my best. This expression can be taken to the extreme when you think about it. Your worse could be when you're sick from the flu and need a lot of help, or it could be when your emotionally unstable and holding a knife to your partner's chest. Those statements shouldn't be used for such extreme behavior with the hopes that someone should excuse you for behaving badly. Learn who you are personally, your character. Change anything that will get in the way of the future you want to have. After that point, you should be working on your emotional intelligence to avoid conflict by not taking most things personally and not being the cause of the war because you are keeping your emotions in check.

I accredit learning this to being the factor that changed my relationship with my child's father. I remember when I initially started working on this area, I would even ask him, "Hey, are you ok? It seems like you are frustrated? Does this have anything to do with me?" Most of the time, he would say, "No, my bad!" It became as simple as asking him that question to resolve frustration. If he said yes, I would ask him what was up? How could we fix it? When you sincerely ask questions, you open the door for answers instead of assuming you already know them.

Get to know why you say and do certain things and how you can respond to keep the peace. Sometimes walking away or hanging up will be helpful. Here is one way to go about hanging up the phone or walking away, with it being a positive move. If a conversation is escalating to an argument that you can't see how to get out of, tell your child's father how you feel: This is frustrating/overwhelming/etc., tell him: I'm not going to argue with you, so let's stop here. If he can't stop arguing, hang up. You can send a text explaining: "I want to hear where you are coming from, and I want to be heard. Let's try again tomorrow." Getting in a yelling match with him isn't going to help.

At the beginning of me working to change how we interacted with each other, it took my son's father and me almost a year of continuously hanging up or blocking the call for a few days to finally get on the same page. In the meanwhile, I had already come to terms with knowing that this transition wasn't going to be easy. So when I wasn't speaking to him, I didn't consume myself thinking about him, the frustration, or what would happen next. I just handled each situation separately and lived my best life in the between time. Self-control will have you avoiding the drama and stop you from being its cause—self-respect and self-love will have you feeling too good to put yourself through the chaos.

4

THE SEE-THROUGH VEIL

Some parents don't talk to their children about why their parents aren't going to be together anymore. I'm not an expert on children's psychology, but I believe this is the wrong approach. Children are a part of the family and are directly affected by your actions. They have feelings and tiny hearts that can break as well. Their unknowing and wondering minds will try to figure out why their parents aren't together. They shouldn't be kept in the dark. Children aren't stupid, and most can handle a gentle approach to this conversation. Don't bad mouth your ex or tell the children way too much information.

"Your father cheated on me!" is not a healthy resolve.

Sitting them down and saying, "We love you, and both want you to know that Daddy and I aren't going to be together anymore," is a healthy way to start. "We will both be here for you, and this is a decision we made for us because we will be happier apart but will support you now and always. You can ask us questions today or any time after you have thought about this. We will answer them to the best of our ability". Is a great way not to over-explain the breakup.

Talk to your kids about their feelings concerning the split. Every conversation should be age-appropriate. Be prepared to be the child's support person. You should never be leaning on your children for support from the breakup. It's not a time to get the child on "your side." It's a time to let the children vent, let them ask questions, and guide them to a state of mind that will allow them to cope with having to accept that you two aren't going to be together. If they need counseling, get them set up quickly. Your child's health insurance, Doctor/Clinic, or Social worker will usually be able to give you some direction on this. Keep reinforcing that the breakup has nothing to do with them. Even a split that happened because you became pregnant is not the child's fault!! It's one or both of the parent's responsibility not to be accountable for their actions. Prioritize your child's feelings and keep their well-being at the forefront of what you say and do. I can't stress this enough.

Mentally healthy children are not children who have never been unhappy, hurt or children whose parents give them everything they wanted. Mentally healthy children are provided with the time, patience, attention, and love to deal with being unhappy about something, hurt by someone, or explained and taught why they don't and shouldn't get everything they want. Doing this will prepare them for life. Let's be honest; the world may disappoint and hurt your child in many ways. Being honest with them and helping them deal with that honesty will show them that they can depend on you.

The older and more mature, the child will appreciate your willingness to talk about important things to them. Doing this allows you to build a bond with your child. They see everything that is going on anyway. They usually don't feel comfortable addressing it with you. Have an open-door policy to let them come to talk when they are ready. I typically probe for conversations I know are on my son's mind to help him open up. You know your children better than anyone else. Have the conversations that need to happen. You are building up good communication skills for your children by doing this. Being the kind of parent that avoids hard conversations doesn't only say a lot about holes in your growth and communication skills but may enable your child to think it's a healthy way of being.

5

NO CROP CIRCLES = NO SIGNS

Once you and your child's father are no longer together, it is in your best interest to set boundaries. Start by keeping your bodies separate! Does this man still love his kids? Most likely, yes! Does that mean you owe him the right to sleep with him for the rest of your life? No! You can no longer sleep in the same bed or give him any reason to think you may give him another chance. He will be looking for signs and body language that you still want him. Avoid giving him the wrong signals at all costs. At this point, you can't do things that you did when you were together. "Being nice" does not always translate as just being nice. He thinks: "she wants to get back together. I may still have a chance!" You have to pay attention to everything you say and do with him now. It's also important to clarify what you mean. If he says or looks like he is taking something you said as you hitting on him, correct it. Not in a mean-spirited way, but say something like, "I can assure you that I am not hitting on you."

From experience, I can tell you that speaking politely to him doesn't always work, but try that first. This man may have convinced himself that you want him back. So every well-mannered or considerate thing you do is flirting or trying to get him back, in his eyes. I have to admit that there did come a time when I was intentionally harsh and cold with my son's father because we weren't making any progress. That may sound weird, but what I mean by that is. As ex's who now had a child together, I wanted to have a smooth transition to co-parenting without being bothered by him trying to hit on me or talking to me about us instead of our son, or without him telling me he didn't want me to date or move on, etc. I genuinely wanted us to be friends who now have a kid and help each other in being good co-parents. I wasn't getting that. I was getting resistance against the breakup and against me moving on because he still wanted to be together.

At first, I tried to keep a good rapport with him, but I shut everything down when that didn't work. I advise that you communicate well and explain what will happen if he doesn't take a hint. I had to explain to him that all the things I did out of consideration will stop. He was either taking it for granted or thought I was flirting, and I needed him to take me seriously. I explained that since I tried to get him on the same page but he wouldn't; I would show him how disconnected I was from him. So, I started by not having small talk anymore. I only spoke about him spending time with our son, what our son needed, and said it in a very straightforward, no-nonsense tone. When he didn't have money to travel, I used to take our son to him, which he didn't appreciate. I stopped doing that. I stopped doing all the things that would make him think I wanted him or was looking for a reason to be near him or speak to him. It still took about a year for him to realize I moved on and needed him to carry his weight and focus solely on our son.

When you plan activities with your child's father, in reality, you are just trying to give your child some memories with both parents. He may see it as wanting to spend time with him. While you are out together with the kids, don't touch each other. Bring your own spending money, sit with your child in between you both, and focus your attention on your child.

The goal isn't to make him jealous or to make him want you back. They say looking and feeling fabulous after the breakup is the best revenge. Months after I left my son's father, I was at an event, and I was standing there 70 pounds lighter, with my new outfit on, feeling better than I did in a long time, and I gave him the eat your heart out facial expression. It was such a priceless moment. Afterward, he called my phone repeatedly, saying he wanted to get back together. It became a headache. Looking and feeling fantastic after the breakup should be a result of focusing on yourself and feeling happy about yourself. So what I am saying is to grow and do better. Don't dangle your new and improved self in front of him with the intention for him to want you so that you can shut him down. Doing things like that will read as you trying to get his attention. You want to be as far away from his notice as possible.

6

SET THE TONE

Boundaries are your best friend when setting the right tone with your ex. If he flirts, ignore it or tell him directly that you would prefer if he stopped. If he calls between 9:30 pm -7 am, don't answer the phone! In the morning, let him know that your child is sleeping at that time, so there is no way he is calling to speak to them. He can talk to them during the hours of 7 am-9:00 pm, or whatever reasonable hours you have previously agreed. No, he can't stay with you while he finds a place because this will put a halt to you moving on. You don't need him there cramping your style anyway. No, you can't be his shoulder to cry on, nor will you accept him calling you to talk about his day or catch up. When you have created boundaries, he respects them, and when they are in place for a while, it shouldn't be a problem to catch up with each other. Otherwise, these are just tricks that men use to keep you from moving on. No kissing for one last time, no touching or any of that! Don't make me sound like the co-parenting police.

The best advice I can give you is to be patient with him. It may take him a while to stop concentrating on you, attempting to get back together, or cease being petty. He may continuously try to get back together, but he will move on one day. His pettiness may be relentless, but give it no attention. The more you argue with him about everything he does or doesn't do. The more he knows that he still matters to you in a romantic capacity. I'm not saying you shouldn't care about what happens to him. You should care because this is the father of your child. There is a difference between caring and making something your problem.

If you were a bank teller, and every other person who comes to your window doesn't have enough money in their account to pay some super important bill. Sure, you may feel like *Dang! I feel bad for that person. I wish I could help*, but you will not hand out your own money to fix everyone's problems. You may even go home after work and think about how bad you felt for that misfortunate older woman who said her grandson stole all her money. Have empathy for your child's father but don't make his problems your own. Someone has to be the bigger person and set the tone for the new kind of interaction you will have. I am challenging you to be that person. It is not an easy job, but your goal as the Super Mom is to do what is best for your child.

When I say to be the bigger person, I'm not saying: let him run all over you or say and do what he desires. Envision a Queen sitting on her throne. She sits there with her head held high, shoulder back, poised. Do you think she would allow a disrespectful person to be in her presence? I don't think so. Would she get loud or leave her throne? I'm sure you know the answer to that. Why does she behave this way? It's because a Queen is sure of who she is. Respect for a Queen isn't demanded; it's required. She doesn't tolerate anyone's foolish behavior, and she knows how to set the tone for her relationships and interactions with people. Now, see yourself as the Queen on her throne. Anytime your child's father or someone else tries to get you to act a fool on your throne, it's your job to set the tone and make the decision to be the bigger person. In this case, that means the more controlled person, the one who doesn't match childish behavior with the same.

If this isn't your typical mode of operation, it will take practice. Your child's father will most likely give you plenty of chances to exercise this new reflex. You have the power to have control of your life and how the future will be with him. Sometimes it will require you to take a walk, take a couple of deep breaths before you reply to that message, or what used to be my favorite: only respond to the parts of a conversation that are appropriate. Set the tone~

Please know that a bitter, controlling, manipulative, or abusive person is not the kind of person who will negotiate. If they do negotiate with you, be wary of their motives. Not only could it be dangerous for you, but it could also be a danger to your child. Ask yourself, will he put you or your child in danger? You need to remove yourself and your child from harm's way as soon as possible if you feel like he will.

7
PETTY IS AS PETTY DOES

It's never a good idea to make your decisions in a petty state of mind. The *Merriam- Webster dictionary defines petty as not very important or severe.

One of the definitions in the urban dictionary defines it as the state of "being" when one does something to annoy someone else. I also loved an example from the Urban Dictionary. It reads: "Florence is so petty she took home all the toilet paper, even the one already on the dispenser, because she was mad that she had no friends, no life, and no clue." Being petty isn't something you have to say or do, but you go out of your way to do it just to spite the other person.

There will be plenty of opportunities to be petty. I advise against taking them. I know, I know! Petty is in right now. Being petty is immature, and doing it while trying to co-parent will lead to drama and bad karma. Karma is very social and jumps from person to person. So given a chance, bad karma will bring itself right back to you in a situation that will not benefit you. Let's say you and your child's father have an arrangement that neither of you will bring people you're not serious about around your child. You find out that he has plans to go out on a date, and you're determined to make him cancel to be petty.

When you think about not picking the child up from your ex, I need you to remember that he may decide to be petty right back. He may let this date come over and spend the time with him and your child. He might even make her answer the door when you finally arrive just to put the cherry on top. He acknowledges that he isn't serious about this woman, but he knows how it will annoy you for him to have her with your child. All this started with a petty decision that now snowballed into a more significant issue. Also, he accomplished his goal. Now you're upset and about to come off of your throne. Was it worth it?

There are some cases where you may respond to your ex, and it just comes out in a petty way unintentionally. Maybe you are having a bad day. It becomes a problem when you realize what you said was petty or he or someone else tells you it was, and you don't take ownership of it even after you have calmed down. Things like that don't just go away. Clear the air, apologize, think about the long-term interaction you want to have with your child's father. Petty and peace are like oil and water; they don't mix. Even if he doesn't accept your apology or doesn't believe it wasn't intentional. Apologize, move on, and be mindful not to do it again. I'm proud of any Super Mom who does this! It means that you have shifted your focus to peace. You are centered on the purpose of all this, which is your child's well-being.

Being petty is a bad character trait. It may feel right at the moment, but the repercussions could be detrimental. Also, it makes for a drama-filled life, and drama can lead to stress. Stress leads to a host of other problems. He may ask if he can skip this weekend with your children. He will make it up by picking them up two weekends in a row next time. As long as he gave you enough notice, it doesn't happen all the time, or it's an emergency, cut him some slack. He may need you to pick up the kids because he is severely sick. Do it this time and ask him to have a backup for next time if you are out of town during his week with the kids or something to that effect. What if he needs two more days to put the child support in the bank because he didn't get paid yet? Are you going to argue about something that he can't change? Why would you do that? It's a waste of your energy.

Just because you are mad, frustrated, or miss him, that doesn't give you the right to keep making the interaction unbearable. All you are doing is becoming why a dad doesn't want to pick up his child. He should not use that as an excuse, but why be a barrier to their relationship for trivial things that can be logically understood? From the examples I gave you, you could easily be in any one of those situations. So, try to put yourself in his shoes.

I remember a time that I was utterly frustrated with my son's father. I was overwhelmed because I felt nothing I was saying or doing made him the father I wanted him to be to our son. Being petty wasn't usually my mode of operation, but the petty thoughts started entering my mind. I think I just wanted him to feel like I did. I wanted him to feel the actual pressures of parenthood. I needed to stop being the one to fix his mistakes and somehow thought being petty would help. I was sure this would allow my son to see him for who he was. I wanted to stop fulfilling his broken promises to our son. I realized, though, that if I did those things and acted out the petty acts that came to mind, I would be letting my son down in ways that could not be forgotten.

During the year our son was eight years old, I found a way to quiet the petty thoughts by no longer expecting anything from my son's father. William Shakespeare said, "expectation is the root of all heartache." He continues to be 100% correct about that, in my opinion. As much as we want to set expectations for others, we have to acknowledge we can't even keep up with every expectation that others have for us or that we have for ourselves. Some of us try harder than others to do and be what is expected of us. Some have a much harder time than others meeting a quarter of the expectations set in their life.

Expectation makes us believe that we have control over anything in life. We don't, and as soon as I accepted this when it pertained to my son's father, I could breathe a little easier. I operated so that I was solely going to be the point person for all things Xavier. I then thought of his father as a helper, not a partner. Proper pressure and responsibility are not put on helpers. So, anything he did was appreciated but not necessary. It was my way of dealing with being the sole provider. I hoped that it would change one day, but I would still hold my son and myself up if it didn't. That's kind of harsh, I know.

Once I was in that mind frame, I had the patience for his father and began to appreciate him more. Once I erased all of my expectations of who he should be and what he should do, I accepted who he was. With that acceptance, I started to use each situation as an opportunity to mature and not concern myself with the things about him that frustrated me. When you learn to have patience with someone who is trying, there is no place for pettiness. We were never going to work as a team for our son until I realized that we would bring different things to the table.

I am stable, dependable, and I offer guidance to his world. His father brought the laidback, learn as you go kind of direction to his life. After eight years of frustration, I discovered that even though the responsibilities were unbalanced. Our son still benefited from having us both. Plus, there were some similarities. We both loved him unconditionally, wanted the best for him, were willing to grow personally to be better for him, and we're where he found comfort. Ultimately, that is what matters.

Don't let anyone tell you differently. When your child's father is doing the best, he can. Don't be petty!

Please don't be petty!!

Sometimes you think the things you do and say are minor nuisances. Those nuisances are usually more significant than they may seem. They can lead to things getting worse. All the negativity you bring to the equation could start building up a wall between your child and their dad. You do not want to be responsible for that.

8

LOOK WHO'S DATING NOW

You have reached a point in your life where you are ready to start dating. Make sure that you do not let your child's father dictate whether you can or not. Also, make sure he is not in the pool of potential partners. Men are territorial; they could have cheated on you 100 times, and still, they will be heartbroken when you start seeing someone else. Stop looking for it to be logical; it's not. There are two reasons I believe a man will have a problem with you moving on. One is they genuinely cared for you and thought they would eventually have their "family back," the other is it's all a game, and making you miserable is part of the fun. The good news is, that's not your problem. You are not responsible for their feelings. They have technically fallen into an "ex-zone."

Just because you have a child with this person doesn't mean they have control over your life after the breakup. Let's pretend for a second that you didn't have a child with this person. They are just an ex-boyfriend. They won't have any say in who or if you date, right? Well, the same applies to your child's father. They are in the "ex-zone," and all ex-zone rules apply to them now.

You are not obligated to tell them when you are ready to date.

When they have your child, don't tell them where you are going because it is not their business. They should only know if it is necessary.

Don't discuss your dates with them or tell them who you are seeing. The only time they should know is when you want your new partner to meet the child. I'm sure you would like to meet the person he has around your child also. It's the responsible thing to do.

From the other perspective: He's dating too.

Dealing with the fact that your child's father has a new significant other that he wants your child to meet is your new challenge. Now that the pettiness is out of the picture, this chapter should be a breeze. Seriously, I'm writing this section from the perspective that you have taken all the other things I already said into consideration, and you agree to implement them. I have never been the mom who meets my ex's new partner. My child's father has met my new partner, and I have met the previous partner of a significant other of mine. Before that took place, we agreed on a few things:

We would need to be with someone seriously for a few months.

They would be a positive influence in our child's life.

We would make sure that we always keep an eye on

how they treat our son and correct anything we don't feel comfortable with.

We never struggled with this part. I have heard and seen other families, friends, etc., go through stress during this conversation, though. The best advice I can offer on this matter is to communicate. Suppose your ex isn't willing to set boundaries. That can lead to your child having to spend more time with you, you speak with their new partner, or you giving your ex some more time to come around on setting the boundaries.

Ultimately, you want to have this conversation at the right time. Don't have it when you're in the middle of an argument. Wait until you are both calm and collected. I suggest you both write down some ideas that you want to discuss concerning significant others and have the conversation over the phone if need be. Do whatever works for your scenario. You don't have to agree on everything. Try to come up with a concise list that works for both of you. The goal should be to set up realistic boundaries and protecting your child from overexposure to multiple partners.

None of your agreements should change just because this new partner wants you to handle it their way. It will be less stressful if you stick to the original deal. Take your time while dating, and make sure you get to know a person before exposing your child to them. Set the example for your child. Be a responsible and mindful dater.

Everyone doesn't have to meet your kid. That goes for both parents. I'm sure you have the best, most adorable kid in the world, but they shouldn't see a revolving door of people coming in and out of either of your lives because you want to show them off. When X was younger, I remember a time where dating was challenging. I didn't have many people I trusted to care for him. I am originally from New York, and I lived in Philadelphia with only my mom living in town. My mom and a few good friends from work would hold me down when I needed a babysitter. This was few and far between because I didn't have time to date. Other than that, it was slim pickings to find a decent man who was kid-friendly.

On one date, a guy said to me that he used to feel like, "I'm not trying to be no step-daddy." I asked him what made him date me knowing I'm a mom. He said, well, he discovered that the women with children are more settled over time, and he wanted that. When I sent him the "dear john" message the next day, he pleaded with me to forgive that comment. He was testing me. To see if I was going to let him be that guy to my kid. I grew up having to deal with that kind of guy as a kid. My mom dated some guys who liked her, but they weren't very fond of me. So, I usually got the short end of the stick. It has always been my intention to protect my son from such an avoidable experience.

There were some guys I dated who wanted to spend more in-person time with me. I communicated to them that I could only function within my free time as a single mom. Here's how the schedule went: My Mother was off from work every other weekend and every other Mon or Thur. I wasn't going to use every free day she had, but she was understanding when I was interested in a person. I would hit up one of my friends if need be, each one only once a month out of four close friends. So if a man was serious about me, he made it work.

When I finally felt comfortable having them meet my son, we would all be together and plan as a family unit. A date was either a 2-3 time a month adults-only event or a trip to a kid's museum, park, dinner, aquarium, or theme park together with our mutual kids. Any man who is rushing to meet your kids or doesn't have patience with a reasonable amount of wait time probably can't handle what you have going on anyway. Who needs that headache?! The right person will understand and work with the situation.

9

YOUR CHILD'S BEST ADVOCATE

Let's face it; no one knows our children the way that we do. When they genuinely have fun, we can see when they are anxious or aren't happy before anyone else. Using your instincts and paying attention to the "tells" that your child shows you are critical. Children aren't usually the best communicators. If you know them like the back of your hand, it will help you understand what they are thinking or what they're going through when they aren't sure if they can verbally express it. Not only were there times where I've seen my son physically express his discomfort in situations where he didn't verbalize it, but when I did notice that, I got him out of there! I tell my son all the time that I have his back! So my actions need to show him that I do, no matter who that affects.

There may come a time when your child's father is not making the right decisions when they are in his care. If he is abusive to your child or refuses to pay child support, and you need it to appropriately care for your child. It would help if you had the court system get involved. I know it's not ideal, but neither is the stress or the trauma that your child could experience. I have mixed feelings about getting involved in the court system. Some people use it in a petty way. For a good dad to be dragged into the system because of pettiness, it looks terrible on his part to be reporting to the child support system through his job. On the other hand, if you feel like no matter how much you talk to your child's father about handling your child's needs and care, he still isn't trying to manage those two things between you both, then there is no way around it.

In my case, as I explained before, I told my son's father to take me to court, but he never did. Please keep in mind that this was my last resort. It was never my goal to separate my son from his father. I know the bond they have, and I tried every other way to get through to my son's father before resorting to separation. There were plenty of other factors that led to this. Once, X's father made the right decisions for our son, even if he wasn't living up to the expectations I had for him. I did not use that as an excuse to separate them. He isn't obligated to live up to my expectations to see his son. Being an advocate for your child sometimes gets misconstrued with taking possession of the child. Possession is a state of owning and controlling something. When advocating means to support, defend, or speak on the behave of a person. When I say being your child's best advocate: I mean that when dealing with anyone but, in this case, your child's father. We should be speaking and acting on our child's behave.

For example, If the child's father doesn't want to give you extra money for a birthday party, you are throwing it at your house, with your family. You decide you are not sending the child over to his father the following weekend for the party he has planned for his family to celebrate with the child. This is not advocating for them; it is possessing them. You control the situation because you can, not because you're acting on the child's behalf. This goes back to the chapter about emotional & personal development. If you have your feelings and character in check, you won't be doing this anymore. You will see that using your child as a pawn isn't about them at all. It's about you because you take pride in having control. That may be a hard pill to swallow. We know the saying: With great power comes great responsibility. When you use your energy positively in combination with self-control, that is when you will genuinely be your child's best advocate.

I realized that I had to be X's advocate, even with his father at times. There were times that he put his own needs and wants before our son. He also blamed me for things that I did or said but didn't like to acknowledge the part he played in why I did them. When he did that, it didn't directly affect our son. I was upset, but I could deal with it. There were times that he told my son things that caused a divide between my son and me. I wouldn't stand for it. Being your child's advocate is a necessary part of keeping their peace of mind, lightheartedness, and overall well-being the highest priority. Do what you need to do (within the law) to keep your child happy and healthy.

Some towns and cities have a designated spot at a police station parking lot or social service center to meet to transfer the child from each parent if you feel you can't deal with the other parent by yourself. Nowadays, there are several ways to receive money without seeing each other (Cash app, Google pay, etc.). So even in extreme cases where you two don't get along, there are still options to make sure the child can have a relationship with both parents and have financial support.

10

STOP! IN THE NAME OF LOVE FOR YOUR CHILD

*I*f I give you a mirror and ask you to look at yourself, you'll only see how you see yourself. You won't see or acknowledge what your child's father sees or what your child sees. I need you to know these other versions of you. When you look at that version, there is a much better chance to fix the things you are doing that prolong progress. If something doesn't apply to you, don't worry about it. Focus on the things that you know you are guilty of and work on them.

Think about some of the things you say and do that push his buttons. Stop doing those things. All jokes aside, this is your child's mentally healthy and happy childhood that is at stake.

Stop thinking about what people will feel when you give your child's father the benefit of the doubt. They don't matter! When you start making positive changes in your life, some people will cut you off because they can't see how their harmful lifestyle will fit your life. This happened to me too. Let them go!

Stop thinking you need to have the last word; you don't.

Stop thinking only you know what your child needs; you didn't bring him into this world alone. Let the child's father share his thoughts and be a part of the decision-making if they make good decisions rooted in their betterment. The more you do this together. The less stress you feel when situations come up. When things happen in my son's life, I can call his dad up and say, please talk to this boy! It feels great to have a partner in parenting.

Stop talking down about your child's father to your child; they may resent you in the future. I'm so grateful my mother didn't do this when I was growing up. My father was mostly absent, but I was able to come to my conclusion about him, and he couldn't blame my mom for it.

Stop making little things into big things. Dad forgot the child's favorite toy at his house but will swing by tomorrow to drop it off. That is not worth a 15-minute argument about how irresponsible he is.

Stop cursing your child out; mature adults don't do that.
*Personal and emotional development

Stop taking out your anger on your child for no reason or any reason. If you had a bad day, leave it at the door or take 20 minutes to decompress before you get your child from daycare.

Stop letting your child have their way as a way to make up

for not fulfilling your dream of providing a two-parent happily ever after. It's not helping them. They need boundaries. Amazingly when you don't give them boundaries, they internalize it as "you don't care enough to take the time to do it."

Stop using your child as an excuse as to why you haven't achieved your goals. Put the child down for a nap and finish your classwork. Whatever it takes, you will both benefit from it in the long run.

Stop avoiding essential conversations. Talk with the child's father about responsibilities being as equal as possible. I honestly don't think they ever will be completely balanced. It's still a good idea to plan out events, responsibilities, and even chores. Do this to avoid either one of you getting burned out. Make a plan for which days either of you will pick up the baby from daycare, which weekends or weekdays they will be sleeping at either of your places. Whose health insurance will the child be on, how will you split monthly costs? Again, realistically I don't believe this will ever be equal, but both of you should make an effort to try to make it as balanced as possible, whether you are together or not. These shouldn't be things that either parent should compromise on for any selfish reason.

If one parent can care for more of the child's needs and the other parent cannot. Then that parent should make sure the child is taken care of no matter what. Ultimately, if you can care for your child on your own and the other parent doesn't want to be in the child's life, then do just that. Take care of them on their own and move on. The damage will happen either way, but by accepting that this person doesn't want to be in your child's life, you can shelter them from the additional damage of having a neglectful parent can cause. If you can't care for the child on your own, remember that you and your child shouldn't go without because a parent doesn't want to be responsible.

Seriously, no matter how young you may have been when you decided that you were mature enough to have sex. You should have also resolved to be mature enough to be a dedicated parent for the baby that came as a result. Even if the child didn't come due to you deciding to have sex, the child is here, so be responsible for them and their needs. Do your healing to be the best mom you can be. I have seen teen parents spring into action when they discover that they will be a parent. Get jobs, finish high school, or even move to a shelter to get their place. If you have made it to this chapter, you have already decided or started to contemplate some of the changes you can make that will change the course of the relationship with your child's father, with your child, and with yourself.

11

WORK SMARTER, NOT HARDER

It takes two people to make a baby because the baby needs both of you. Both of you bring something invaluable to the table. Once you accept that, things will work out a lot easier for both of you. Working against each other ends up cutting out a helping hand. It's a wiser idea to join forces and help each other get through parenthood with a little less grey hair.

Raising my son as a single parent was far from easy. At one point, I was paying more for childcare than I was for my monthly rent. Taking off work to be at his shows, Saturday morning baseball, soccer, and basketball games or practice was exhausting sometimes. My son struggled with things that were stressful for me to deal with alone. Most days, I didn't feel like I knew what I was doing. I was doing the best that I knew how. Those are only a handful of things that would have been easier if I had the full support of his father and made more intelligent decisions when he was younger.

I wish someone would have told me the things I'm telling you. I didn't have the best examples to follow growing up. Even so, I knew I didn't want to follow what I saw. At the time, I didn't have the knowledge I needed to make smarter decisions. I didn't know enough about life. I didn't realize how much our "childhood" can shape our whole life. I know you want the best for your child. Please listen to me when I say. Healthy co-parenting is smarter than intentionally working against each other. It's more beneficial for your life, body, mind, and child's well-being.

When I see married friends or co-parents tag team parenthood, it puts a massive smile on my face. I can see how much both parents benefit from having each other—getting the night off because the child is spending it at his dad's house. Yes, please! The baby won't fall asleep, so you sleep from 8 pm to 2 am, and your partner sleeps until 2 am- 8 am; Yesss! It's those little moments of relief that help you get by sometimes. If the other parent can be involved, let them! Set an example for your child. Show them how adults handle their responsibilities and that adults work together for the greater good even when they don't want to be together.

In the long run, to your child, it doesn't look like Mommy took off from work to be present at my show this week, and Daddy took off from work last week to attend my soccer game. To them, it looks like constant love and support.

Working smarter may be hard to do when you don't have clear *agreed-upon expectations of each other's responsibilities and roles. It's a great practice that once you decide on things. Put them in writing. You start by writing down the who, what, where, why, when, and how's of things that need to happen regularly and then review and update it as things come up. People forget things! There is probably nothing my son's dad hated more than me reminding him of what he didn't do. So having it written down or programmed in a phone and organized will help to avoid conflict.

Example:

Dad's list

- Every other Fri, Dad picks up the child and has her until Sunday afternoon.
- Dad will buy his diapers, wipes, clothes, and baby food that he keeps at his house.
- Dad will pay the child care bill when he picks up the child every other Friday from the childcare center.
- (write out dates)
- Dad will take the child to a barber/hair salon every two weeks or once a month.
- Dad will attend all morning school performances since he works at night.

Mom's list

- Every other Friday, Mom will make sure she dresses the child appropriately when Dad picks her up.
- Mom will attend any school performances in the

afternoon because she works evenings and can take off when needed.
- Mom will make sure to style her daughter's hair while in her care and before she leaves for her father's house for the weekend if he doesn't know how to do it.
- Mom will pay the childcare bill every other week on Fri when she drops the baby off at the childcare center. (write out dates)

These aren't super hard things to write out, and you'd be surprised how one parent could think the other parent is going to the school performance, but it's their turn. How you bring up this list is essential also. Don't bring them up as chores. Make sure not to use a parenting tone (I made this mistake all the time). Respect that you both will forget something and thank each other for sticking to the agreement when things are going well. You don't even have to write it out together. Send your list in an email. They can reply with theirs and agree to meet in the middle (Using a google doc that can be edited by you both can work also). Text messaging a quick reminder doesn't hurt either. You could even have a shared calendar to keep track of things. Don't overthink the process. Make it and stick to it!

12

ASK AND TELL

You made it this far, and you still want answers to more scenarios? Here are some situations that I may not have covered and solutions to handle them. My answers are based on putting you and your child first. There are probably plenty of other explanations for these scenarios, but these are my go-to solutions.

1. When the child is with you, they eat fried chicken and French fries. When they are with their dad, they eat baked chicken and vegetables. You both argue about what you want the child to eat when you are with your child.
Answer: This issue is not a personal attack on your cooking, and it isn't about either of you. It's about the child. It's about doing what is best for them. Make the healthy meals you know how to make, and you can stop arguing and feel good about what your child is eating at all times. If one of you doesn't

know how to cook, maybe suggest some quick meals, print out some recipes that are easy to follow, or recommend some restaurants that have healthy options. Some parents even send the child food to eat at the other parent's house for the weekend. I know, I'm reading your mind: *Irene! That's too much!*

Some parents do this. Sometimes you're at your wit's end, and you need to accept the other parent isn't going to get on board. The goal is still what's best for the child. Find a balance.

2. During the school week, you send the child to bed at 8:30 pm. Their father lets them stay up until they want to go to bed.
Answer: Have a sit-down and have an explanation as to why you both want to keep your house rules about bedtime. Do not judge each other's ideas! Give examples of why it would benefit the children to go to bed at a set time during the school week. Ex: They need to be well-rested for school. Find ways to compromise. Ex: There doesn't need to be an agreed-upon bedtime on the weekends. If both of you can get to a point where you aren't acting out of pettiness, you should be able to reach an agreement. Last resort, you speak to the child directly about making the right decisions. My go-to was to keep my son on such a strict bedtime routine that even when he wasn't with me, he would fall asleep at his regular time anyway.

3. You aren't ready to date, and your child's father is the last

person or the only person with whom you've ever had sex. Should you ask them to have sex with you in the meanwhile?
Answer: No! Continuing to have sex with each other after breaking up and attempting to be friends with benefits is a terrible idea. It will lead to drama and make a mess of the structure and boundaries you are supposed to be putting in place.

4. Your child's father calls you at 11:00 pm and says he wants to spend the night with your child at your house. What do you do?
Answer: Say No! Doing this is not keeping your child from their father. It's an example of setting boundaries. If he wants to spend the night with the child, he can pick them up at an appropriate time and have them sleep over with him at his house. If he doesn't have a comfortable space for them where he is currently staying, your child's father needs to be concentrating on doing what he needs to employment-wise and education-wise to afford his place.

5. Your child's father calls you at 2:00 am to talk. What should you do?
Answer: Don't answer the phone and turn the ringer off. Set your boundaries! The next time you talk to him. Let him know that it is unacceptable for him to call you at that time. Give him a set time for the latest and the earliest that he can contact you. Booty call hours are not acceptable! Keep in mind that he may just be calling at that time in the morning to annoy any potential partners that are there.

6. How to decide rewards and punishment for the child?
Answer: Your child should be earning their rewards. The rewards and punishments should be agreed upon by both of you. Unfortunately, there is no easy answer to this one, and you may never find common ground. In my experience, my son's father and I were on the same page about it. We struggled with him not being consistent with how he gave rewards and punishments, but once he saw how it negatively affected our son's progress, we were back on the same page. Hopefully, you guys can learn from our mistakes on this one and do what is best for your child.

7. Your child's father has the child for the weekend. He doesn't have any money to pay for any activities or buy out for dinner. He asks you for funds to make sure they have a good weekend. What should you say?
Answer: No! As long as he has food in the house, they will eat. He should be planning his money out in advance for the time he has with the child. You are not responsible for either of those things while the child is in his care. If he doesn't have any food, of course, your child should be staying home.

8. You are at home, and you hear a knock at the door. It's your child's father. He stopped by because he wanted to see the kids. What should you say?
Answer: You need to explain to him that he needs to call first when he expects to see the child. This is about boundaries! He should not be allowed to come into your space unannounced.

If you follow the answers I gave you above, it will help you start to build a drama-free co-parenting existence. They will take time to get adjusted. You may get some resistance, but it's worth it in the end. All the answers aren't here because there is no master text with all the answers to co-parenting. Things will be different for everyone, and there will be situations that we can't foresee. It's up to you guys to remember that every decision you make will affect your child. So every time you say or do something, keep them in mind.

They are the innocent bystanders in the situation, and since you brought them into this world, you should be doing your best to make it a pleasant experience for them. I didn't say perfect, but at least as enjoyable as you can. It should also be your goal to show your children how good co-parenting looks. My mother always used to say, "Do as I say, not as I do." That worked for me, but it doesn't for everyone. I was able to learn from other people's mistakes to avoid stress and drama. For the most part, children watch their parents and use what they do or don't do as guides for life. Be the kind of person you want them to become. You are not the average BabyMama out here doing all kinds of nonsense. Make the type of decisions you would like your child to make. They are watching!

13

CO-PARENTING HAVEN

A co-parenting haven is a safe place that provides refuge from the storms of parenthood. Reaching a point where you are willing to co-parent in peace will take different amounts of time for everyone. If you haven't gotten to this point, let me give you a sneak peek into this world. At this current point in time, my son is 17 years old. He lives with me during the school year and spends almost all of the school breaks with his father. Also, they call each other whenever they want; his father sends child support monthly when our son is with me. They play Xbox with each other online since we live a couple of states away from each other.

We bring things to each other's attention about our son. We talk to each other about what's bothering him or what excites him. We both meet his needs emotionally and financially. When we disagree, we talk calmly without disrespecting each other. We hear each other out until we agree. We don't discuss our disagreements with our son. When he tells me he can't do something we decided on, one of my habits is to say to him: "I believe in you," the truth is, I do believe in him. After all of the growth we have had to get here. I have no reason not to think that he will work things out and get them done.

It is such a peaceful interaction that I never thought we would have. It's so much easier for us to focus on our son since we are less worried about each other. I accept that his father is doing "his best" to be better for himself and our son. We verbalize to each other the efforts that make the difference in making our partnership work. I much appreciate him, and we are friends. We even talk to each other about how things are going in our personal lives. We encourage each other and stand together during times that we need to get our son on track. It's not perfect. It's what I have worked hard to accomplish; it brings us both peace and a partner in parenthood.

What's so interesting is people who only know of us from the last four or five years can't fathom that we were ever at odds. They think that when I talk about how challenging this process was upfront, it couldn't have been so bad if we are where we are now. It's a testament to the work we put in. On the opposite end, people who knew my son's father and me way back when. Know the real deal and can attest to the progress. I used to think I would explode with anger and frustration regularly when on the phone with Xavier's dad. My common phrase was: he is aggravating my soul! Time didn't just magically change us; we did.

14

NEVER-ENDING PARENTHOOD

Parenting is an amazingly rewarding struggle. The Lord blessed me with a son. Did I think it was the right timing? No. Did I think it was the right man? No. The older I got, the more I realized that everything does happen for a reason. I learned so much about real love from being a Mother. I learned so much about myself from managing my relationship with my son's father. I no longer question God's timing. I'm just grateful for the opportunity to be my son's mother.

I take that responsibility very seriously, and since you read this book to the end, I know your taking co-parenting seriously too. I hope that you learned something.

Something was always happening in my life or around me to other co-parents that gave me more to add to this book. Many people around me are still struggling with co-parenting. It gave me even more motivation to cover as much as I could. My goal was to ensure that my friends, family, and you are given my best ideas and examples of my worse behavior to avoid. Helping you reach the co-parenting haven is all I want. I pray that this book gives you the motivation to make changes, be the best Super Mom you can be, and let people know you're not the average BabyMama because of it.

Made in the USA
Columbia, SC
27 June 2021